H The
eart
of the
Initiate

Also by Victor H. Anderson:

Thorns of the Blood Rose
Etheric Anatomy (with Cora Anderson)
Lilith's Garden

Also by Cora Anderson:

Fifty Years in the Feri Tradition
Etheric Anatomy (with Victor Anderson)
Childhood Memories
Kitchen Witch: A Memoir
In Mari's Bower: A Biography of Victor H. Anderson

H The eart
of the
Initiate

Feri Lessons

SECOND EDITION

Victor and Cora Anderson

HARPY
BOOKS

Portland, Oregon

Published by Harpy Books,
an imprint of Acorn Guild Press
4207 SE Woodstock Blvd # 168
Portland, OR 97206-6267
USA

Cover art: Michele Jackson

Contents

Foreword.. v

Acknowledgments...vii

SOME PICTISH VIEWS ON THE OLD RELIGION 1

COMMENTARIES...11
    Raised to the Power of Divinity 13
    Sexual Initiation... 15
    Sexual Ethics 17
    Training and Initiation... 19
    The Consort 21
    The Guardians.. 23
    The Morning Prayer 25
    The Black Heart of Innocence............................... 27
    Possession 29
    Salvation 31

LETTERS TO STUDENTS... 33
    Written by Cora, March 20, 1996:
    to a new student, the Ha Prayer, Kala Rite,
    Eclecticism, Her Background 35

    Written by Cora, July 31, 1994:
    the Dual Consort, the Guardians, the Nephilim,
    the Purpose of the Circle, Casting the Circle.................37

    Written by Victor:
    Vodou, the Nature of the Great Goddess........................ 39

    Dictated by Victor, February 13, 1992:
    his background, Blue Fire, the Star Goddess, the
    Points of the Pentagrams, the Blue God, Arddhu,
    Nimue, Mari, Anna, the Triune Soul, the Secrets of
    the Craft, Poppets and Paper Boats, the Path of the
    Heart, Woman's Power, Power and the Pentagrams,
    the Story of the Ninja Warrior, Witchcraft 43

Dictated by Victor, April 18, 1992:
the Martial Nature of Feri, the Black Goddess,
the White Goddess, Colors and Symbols 63

A PRAYER FOR THE CRAFT NEOPHYTE 73
Prayer for Beginning the New Path 78

Foreword

THIS BOOK IS A VALENTINE from Victor and Cora Anderson to you. For those of us who are their initiates, the Andersons live on through the many personal recordings and letters we hold close and treasure. We're grateful for this opportunity to share rare insights into the Andersons' teachings, and offer you an intimation of what it was like to be their student.

Victor Anderson was a taskmaster. He took pride in testing his students. I recall him grilling me on the meaning behind a story he told about a missionary who visits Tahiti and refuses flowers from a beautiful woman. After carefully considering Victor's words, I finally spoke up that it was about the missionary declining to make love to the woman, and thus refusing her the gift of a child. Victor beamed. I was always happy to please him with a correct response.

I'll never forget the sensation of Victor putting me under the protection of Oro. Victor directed me to create a small spear and tie bright red feathers to its dull end. When I had completed this task, he held the spear, sharp tip up, and declared it was time for the ceremony to begin. I knelt before him as he leaned forward in his rocking chair, carefully aiming the spear above my head. The ceremony was brief but powerful. I could feel heat radiating from the core of my body. When I told him how warm I felt, he laughed. "It means it worked," he said.

The vision that Cora had that rainy afternoon was equally powerful. During the ceremony, she said she saw a beautiful man standing in a tree, with brilliant, long feathers dangling from his torso. Victor smiled and said that that was Oro. Cora was delighted by this vision, and I felt privileged to be in their company and under Oro's protection.

The details of that memory were nearly lost until last month, when I transcribed the recording we have of that afternoon. Listening closely, I was transported back to their living room, felt their presence, and heard the rain pattering outside.

When Victor passed away in 2001, Cora was devastated, yet she endured, found her inner resolve, and faced her challenges with a sharp wit and a delicious sense of humor. Although Cora was bedridden as a result of a stroke she suffered in 1998, she was determined to see her husband's poetry back in print. She had a keen insight few possess. I quickly learned to turn to her for advice on life, the Craft, and how best to present their literary works. I still feel like I can consult her, and I am confident she helped inspire this book's production in her own way, from the other side of the veil.

I hope *The Heart of the Initiate* offers its reader a taste of what it was like to study under the Andersons. It's often said that the difference between what they taught their initiates and what they taught the occasional visitor was distinguished by the depth of the material the Andersons delivered. As witness to them teaching both parties, I can say that this is true. This book provides a glimpse into the heart of Feri as Victor and Cora Anderson knew it. Gaze carefully, for as Victor often said, we are a martial tradition. And remember Cora's advice: never, ever give your power away.

—Jim Schuette
February 1, 2010

Acknowledgments

Thanks to
Onyx and Anaar, Corvia Blackthorn,
Lawrence Carroll, and Michele and Leroy
Jackson for their help producing this book.

SOME PICTISH VIEWS ON THE OLD RELIGION

Some Pictish Views on the Old Religion

by Victor H. Anderson Δ. Σ. Τ.

I REALIZE ONLY TOO CLEARLY just how fragmented the Craft has become in recent years since the revival started, as many believe, by G. B. Gardner and his school of magical and religious thought. At the present time the Craft, as it is in the public eye, has taken on a largely Celtic flavor and, in some traditions, a rather puritanical cast. This may be due to the fear of the wrong popular image and the starting of another wave of churchly propaganda and outright persecution. Many of them seem to me to be afraid to come out and be real Witches. They do not want to antagonize the power structure and make themselves useful in the affairs of our country. They prefer to look as white as possible. In the types I now speak of, they sit on the fence and crow about how magic is to be used only for good. We are told that if anyone steps on us and we hit back, it will return threefold whether we are right or wrong. As we all know, Celts are fighters and claim to be ever ready to lay their lives on the line for freedom and justice. Why then do some so-called white Witches insist on being of Celtic

3

traditions? This kind of "white Witch" is afraid of sex and what is called Black Magic. She is like the woman who says: "I didn't get married just for THAT!" Great lengths are gone to in order to deny things that any really initiated Witch knows her Craft sisters and brothers are doing right now and have been doing for ages. Now that I have finished my rather negative approach, I will try to speak briefly for my branch of the Craft.

As my position places certain grave responsibilities upon me, I do not wish to be misunderstood as condemning all those who call themselves white Witches. I am thinking of those who are very sincere, especially those who are new in the Craft. Being known as white can protect one at times, from being accused of psychic malpractice, a term much better than the derogatory use of the words "Black Magic," when they are used to describe really evil things done in our name. It is stupid to throw away our weapons because some cults of evil use them to commit vile atrocities. We do not condemn all medical instruments because of quackeries and septic abortions. Would it make sense for a Witch to refuse to become a doctor for fear of the dangerous knowledge placed in her hands? That could only be called one thing—shirking one's responsibilities.

My purpose in writing this article is not so much to grind an ax as to put forth our desperate need to survive as a potent force in shaping the future of our age. We are in need of much more learning about the real nature of our Craft and how to use it. I do not mean that we are by any standards ignorant in what we do. Under all the publicity, there is a hard core of old-fashioned Witches of several traditions including my own, the Fairy or Pictish, who are trying to get it together again. It is difficult to realize the damage done during the persecution. Much has already been written concerning the history of Witchcraft, and much of it is good. However, I should add a few brief comments on what my tradition has to say on this subject. We should not try to pinpoint the exact place of its origins. Like poetry, which has always been a part of it, the Craft sprang up in many places and among several races as a natural part of the human experience.

According to my tradition, first there were the shamans who were of both sexes and often homosexual. These mysterious people were very necessary to the tribe or group of which they were a part. They possessed unusual powers to communicate with the spirits and Gods and with the most ancient of Deities, the Great Goddess, who was the most dominant and powerful force in the majority of prehistoric religions. These conditions applied to a large portion of human kind in the far distant past, yet they are not the entire story.

The family of those days usually consisted of a mother and her children. Fatherhood was not generally recognized or understood as of any importance. This was the premarital state of humanity. We lived in the tribal state or in small bands. The small band was a kind of group marriage where the female was dominant. In this respect we were more feline than primate. Our other relatives never made it out of the forests and humid jungles but stayed behind, never attaining humanhood. On the other hand, among the protohumans there were individuals who were already beginning to be looked up to for their extra-instinctual or extrasensory powers, and so our Craft began to emerge. Even these protohumans loved, feared, hated and, yes, even dreamed. Since their growing minds were not yet trash baskets for Freudian garbage due to sexual repression, they soon found that during sleep they could leave their bodies and float about through the forest. This, and the awareness of an omnipresent female power were the beginnings of all religion!

In these dreams they met discarnate tribal members and came to know of survival. Because of the above-mentioned simplicity of mind, they also found it easier to remember past lives, and so was born the knowledge of reincarnation. My tradition does not believe that the fear of ghosts came until much later.

At this point it becomes necessary to speak briefly of one of the oldest and most astounding beliefs held among my people. According to this legend the first and greatest civilization on our planet was that of "The Mothers." For many years I have been trying to discover enough facts on which to base at least a personal opinion of their original appearance and color. Although the Wee Folk were rather dark, they seemed to favor the following description: a race of beautiful women with fair skin, blue or green-blue eyes, and reddish-golden hair. They were 5 feet tall but very strong and agile. They were slender and finely made but tough and wiry. They excelled in physics, music, and magic. The method of reproduction was parthenogenetic, "but they excelled the pupils of Sappho in the arts of sexual joy." I am here quoting a Greek Witch under whom I had the privilege of studying briefly (she was tiny and dark and could have passed as one of my own racial ancestors). She told of yet another Greek tradition that says "The Mothers" were blue-skinned and, in fact, were the parents of that almost forgotten people, the Wee folk, before they became men and women.

I have been told other things by various races. Certain Germans have given me the first description except for height, which they gave as 5 feet 8 inches. Racial preferences are easily discernable especially in the Germanic image. But aside from the small stature attributed to them by both Mediterranean, Scottish/Irish people who share my racial heritage, The Mothers are pictured either as a race of fair women or the original Blue Race. In Polynesian legends they are lovely blondes. But if, as my people believe, humankind originated in Africa, perhaps, this very ancient parthenogenetic race was originally black! If so—and this is a personal opinion—they held within their wombs the primal seeds of all races and colors. But I can find arguments against this theory. In France, a hazy form of this ancient lore is still to be found. I quote from *The School of Venus* by Michel Millot and Jean L'Ange. It was first published in Paris in 1655. Susanne says to her cousin, "Well, you have to remember this. Once upon a time men and women formed a single body, joined together at the genitals, the man's being enclosed within the woman's, so that men never died but reproduced themselves continually by that part of them which was their wives, thus escaping death . . ." In spite of the fact that this is a playfully wholesome manual of erotic love, we have yet another clue as to ancient folk memories. Among the remnant of the Fairy Race now scattered about the world, some say white, some say blue, for the color of the race championed by Elizabeth G. Davis in *The First Sex*.

Even though there was an older civilization that had already begun to decline while other *Homo sapiens* were still developing in Africa, I think it safe to conjecture that the same general rules apply to the growth of Witchcraft. We have already spoken of the Old Religion predominant in prehistoric times. In my tradition we believe Witchcraft developed through the formation of secret medicine lodges within the framework of the older religion of the people. Shamans began to find ways to work together, first in pairs, then in groups. In the formation of the Witch-pair lies the primal root of marriage as the white races see it today, regardless of its present flaws. It would seem that the coven would evolve naturally from this point and in some cases probably did. However, a much older form of it was already in existence. It was made up of nine bisexual women who were the orgiastic priestesses of the Goddess. When they saw what was happening in the medicine lodges, they took a hand in building the coven of female-male couples presided over by a priestess or priest. The first groups were not limited to thirteen. It was discovered early in the Craft that thirteen people doing a working together produced the best results. If a couple grew tired, the Circle was opened and another took their place after being sprinkled with blood or charged water, then the Circle was closed. This sprinkling was done with a phallus-shaped aspergill [*sic*] of some root, possibly a wild carrot.

These ancient folk were as free and uninhibited as pre-Christian Polynesians. But because some members preferred to work in semi-monogamous pairs, there developed what my tradition calls the Red or Blue Rite, or the red or blue coven. A red coven is similar to group marriage. At the time of this writing, they would be called "swingers," though I dislike this term because of its connotations of male chauvinism and frivolity. A blue coven is one in which couples work as units, as at a dance where married folks do not change partners. Even in blue groups, red rites are sometimes done when necessary or desired. Some are able to work in both ways. We must not be squeamish. This has been known for many years among anthropologists and students of Witchcraft, both pro and con. The colors are just now being mentioned in my tradition after a long silence, as far as I know. So far, only white and black are bones of contention. We must stop being so afraid of public opinion. Ours is the oldest religion of the so-called common people, and it has been my personal experience that they much prefer the real thing to the whitewashed imitation, in a deep and very sincere way. We must give ordinary humans credit for having hearts and brains together with decency, once they find what they most need.

The Pictish Tradition has several theological and ritual similarities to several others, but there are some differences, which I feel it is now permissible to point out. I hope these differences will not cause disharmony any more than certain religious variations among tribes of Native Americans. Although the Craft I follow is originally that of the Little People of Scotland and Ireland, there are elements of ancient Greek, pre-patriarchal Jewish beliefs as well as strong, deep spiritual ties with the Vodoun rites and beliefs of the black peoples. It is not likely, however, that a noninitiate would recognize some of these things in what they might be allowed to see, but a mambo or houngan would quickly understand. My foremothers and priests were quite eclectic. Like the Romani, they took what they found and used and shaped it to their needs without losing its originality and native intelligence.

In common with most other traditions, we worship the Great Goddess. For us, God is a Woman, having within Her all principles, powers, and potencies of Nature. Mari and Krom are the non-secret names of our Blessed Lady and Her Consort, Herself, and Her Other Half (see *Aradia, the Gospel of the Witches*, page 18). The sacred Bull and upright Phallus are prime symbols of this beneficent but sometimes terrible potency. There are seventy-one Gods in constant attendance upon Her, from which She chooses twelve as a high inner council. From these She may elect a Secondary Consort, acting with Krom and in His image. This is the original idea behind the "seventy-two names of God."

We believe in the Great Rite. We do it for its own sake as a natural and joyous act of adoration to The Lady and our old Nature Gods. The fact that it is the quickest way to raise power is a truth we do not need as an excuse for performing it. Parts of this rite are very secret, but this much can be said: when people truly love and respect one another, all things are done decently and in order. There is a tender beauty and holy majesty in the Great Rite that brings out the very best in us as human beings. By the very nature of our religion, we could never do anything to upset or demean the dignity and glory of Woman, nor of either sex in our ceremonies.

In my tradition we do not quibble over whether magic is black or white. As we define it, all magic that really works is "black." The life force and bioplasma exuded from our naked or robed bodies is as dangerous as sulfuric acid, in the hands of the patriarchal or nonreligious magician. My people believe poetry to be the true White Magic, called "white" in honor of The Lady as Muse, or Moon Goddess. It can be cutting and deadly too! Black covers everything else, from mediumship to tellurgy, whether used for healing or killing, peace or war. I know this has been said many times before, but I say it from personal experience, being myself a male Witch. My religion is a fine and beautiful thing. But if you value your sanity and even your life, *do not play games with it*!

COMMENTARIES

Raised to the Power of Divinity
... from Victor

There is a saying,

> The Holy One loves us with the same love
>> with which we love one another,
>> but raised to the power of divinity.
> It is older than law.
> It is older than reason. ...

It's one of the basic tenets of our religion. The Gods and spirits are real creatures, not just concepts or ideas.

Sexual Initiation
... from Victor

We are a sex positive tradition, but you must know the heart of the one you approach. No one must ever be approached with force or poor intent.
—Victor Anderson, 2001

We do not consider sex an "aspect" of something. It's not just important because it's something on the side; it's just what it is. And it is not unlawful to have sex to initiate somebody. But it must be that person's choice. If you don't have love for that person, and they don't have love for you, what's the use? We have a saying among the Apache Indians, "A woman in your arms but not in your heart is like looking at yourself in a mirror while sleeping on a bed of rocks."

This is one thing that I wish I could make clear to people. Full rite initiation has to be an act of love just as if you're marrying somebody or going with them. It's got to be somebody you care enough about. And if they are not willing to be initiated in that way, we have a ceremony called the Intentions of the Heart. ...

Yes, we do initiate that way. It's no different and no more shameful than for people to be sexually active before they get married. But they must be with the right person, and a right time, and a right place for a relationship. We do not throw ourselves around.

It's not because we consider sex as something rotten or something wrong. It's because we consider it so important, because that's how the Goddess created the universe. When the big bang came, that was a sexual orgasm just as truly as when we have one. The same feeling.

It's no different than, say, if you go to live with somebody, you mate with them, and you unite with them. But if you are doing this for other purposes and you already have a lover, or if you wish to wait, we have the Intentions of the Heart. Because that's what counts.

We do this ceremony, and then we tell them,

> Let your next act of love be the sealing of your vows to the Goddess, to our Lady, and the Consort, whether this person be or be not of our religion, so there is love.

And that's what we say at the end of the ceremony. And then we add,

> If you cannot in this life,
> let it be known that you will in the next.

Sexual Ethics
... from Cora

As far as the Craft goes, I don't know if anybody will listen to any of this. Maybe there are a few good people out there, but I don't know. Anyway, most of the people, in the beginning and maybe still, thought sex was a wonderful thing. You shouldn't just throw it away, anyway you want. I said, "Don't ever throw it with me. If you do, you'll get sent back with it." And they never did bother me, they didn't dare. I said to Victor, "If anybody ever comes on to me, I'm just gonna tell them where to get to." And he said, "You do that and it'll be all right." I thought they'd quieted down about it, but evidently not, from the stories I've been hearing.

There are ethics to the Craft. Don't go off into evil stuff; learn to do something good. The Craft is about loving one another and doing right by everyone you see. Do right by them. Even if they don't agree with you, and they do you wrong, you do right by them. Then, if they do something you don't like, you just tell them, "I don't believe in that. I don't do it, and I won't do it." We believe that the Craft is a very good thing. It's a solid foundation if anyone gets the right teachings and they do the right thing. I know some people don't like it when I say that, but it's true. If they live as long as I have, they'll find out about it.

The Craft is a sexual religion, but we behave ourselves and do it in a way that is right. And it's not right to go with other men or other women and throw on them when you are supposed to conduct yourself in an orderly way when you go among them. At least that's the way we believed. But everybody has their own idea. I always said the Craft would not last because of that kind of behavior. That's what will destroy the Craft if they don't do right.

Training and Initiation
... from Cora

I hear a lot of talk about who is able to initiate. Who can do that?

I'll tell you, I've come to a conclusion about initiation. Anybody who has been in the Craft and has gone on a long time and knows they're a good report, they're eligible to initiate. You don't want to initiate just anybody. And don't do a thing if a person is going to run after children. Be careful. And we ask them certain questions at home. I know it sounds hard, and some people may not be able to get into it. It's not other religions' rules. In other words, Feri is more lenient in some ways. In other ways, it's not.

So you don't need to study with someone for a long time?

No. You could come as a stranger. My husband would ... Someone would come to him right out of the blue. And he'd say, "Let's see," and ask some questions first—some pretty pointed questions. Then they'd ask, "Well, can I be initiated?" And he'd answer, "You come back here for several times and study with me, and then you can be initiated." And that's what he did. I don't say he didn't make mistakes. With some people I believe he may have. He said, "No, but they haven't cleaned themselves up right." Now initiation nowadays, I don't understand these people. Nowadays they say you've got to do seven years with somebody, which isn't true. We did require one woman to come and study with us for a year and a day, and she turned out to be one of the better people that I know of in the Craft.

There's no set time limit to study?

No, there's no time limit. Some people are kind of like myself ... When I was young, a little fairy visited me one time. He said, "Cora, I love you, you've been a good girl. I'll show you where there's a nickel on a rock bluff. And you take that nickel and buy yourself some candy." So the next morning I went on to school and I came to this rough bluff, and sure enough there was a nickel. So I went to school and bought some candy. There are things like that. I saw many things. People would lose things, and I could find them for them. They'd ask me where they were, and I'd say they're in so-and-so place in your house, or they're out under this rock or this tree. I knew that, and there are people who are like that. It doesn't take long for them to study about the Craft. I was just very fortunate to marry Victor. Otherwise I don't think I would have married anybody if it hadn't been for him.

The Consort
... from Victor

There was a time long ago, when God Herself and her Consort were simply called God together. And God above and
God below. And the Consort is the same person that Christians later made into the Devil, or Satan,* because they had
to get rid of him, because they felt there was too much sex
and violence and too much nature. They gave themselves
away by making him into the image of what they had of a
wild thing. They really crippled themselves. They took one
of his real names to make him into something vile, just like
Hitler misused the swastika. Actually, "Sétan" is not the
name of an evil spirit at all, but the Consort. So Christians
go around calling their spirit "evil," just because in a back-
handed way they seal him up into a very twisted sadomasochistic god.

That same person—whom they have denied, defiled,
and messed up as the Devil in Christianity—is really Sétan,
the Consort of the Lady herself—the great Lucifer,† Melek
Ta'us, King of Many Colors, Bright Spirit. He was brought
forth from the divine lust of God Herself. This must be understood. They really are the divine parents.

---

* "Satan represents the repressed sexual cravings of Christians" (Victor Anderson, via Michele Jackson, January 7, 2001).

† "Lucifer was never the Devil. It's a big lie" (ibid.).

The Guardians
... from Victor

Would you tell us about the Guardians?

The Guardians are four spirits that come and join your coven whenever you have a ceremony. They're all around us. They are among the Gods, in the air, all about us. They each take the name of one of the four great Cosmic Gods. The Great Ones are therefore the Guardians of your coven. But it's useless to say ... what one coven calls "*the* Guardians" are the only ones there are, because if you have seven or eight hundred covens in the world having ceremonies, you're going to have seven or eight hundred quadruplets of Guardians.

They're like the Loa. Because Vodou is really the heart of all religion in a way. People don't realize that though. All our ancestors walked out of Africa long ago, and really did seed the races of all people. That's where we all come from.

The Morning Prayer
... from Cora

Would you talk about the morning prayer?

Sometimes in the morning, something's on your mind from the day before. Maybe you had to do something. So you get up and say to yourself that you'll have a good day, that things will go right for that appointment and everything, and that all three selves be straight within you. I always say that after every prayer.

What other kinds of exercises would you recommend to people?

I think walking is good, and meditation. You should meditate as you walk. Try to walk among oak trees, or other trees, if you can. Of course, studying. If you write, writing. Some people don't do too much of anything, some people do a lot. I think to be really good and devoted, you have to stay with prayer and meditation. That way you learn things.

The Black Heart of Innocence
... from Victor

What is the Black Heart of Innocence?

In the Feri Tradition, and in Celtic Witchcraft, but especially the Feri Tradition, there is a saying:

> How beautiful is the black lascivious
> purity in the hearts of children and
> wild animals.

Now that is a clue as to what the Black Heart of Innocence is—that sexual purity that exists in the child before she or he has been battered into submission by corrupted adults. It is just as pure as the urge of a plant to reach toward light. And that is something that we have lost in the human race as a whole. And stories like that in Christianity about the Garden of Eden—where sex is made into the original sin, and everything is blamed on woman, and blamed on the serpent—is just an example of how old this loss is. And just how burdened humans are with being, in effect, and in fact, a sex cripple. Because that is what most human beings are: sexual cripples. They don't have that sweet innocence any longer.

And when they found it in the Polynesian lands, such as when Captain Cook went to Tahiti, they called it fornication and sin, and so on. It's not as simple as it might seem. Yet, in another way it is very simple. A child could understand it, if you presented it to the child in the right way. So that's the real meaning. Most adults are very much afraid of this. A poet and a mystic of our kind can understand the meaning of the Black Heart of Innocence.

The Black Heart or Black Rose of Innocence is sometimes symbolized by a black fish, or a flower that reminds one of a black geranium. There are those who equate the Black Heart of Innocence with the "clean slate," but no, that is not what it means. Now if someone wishes to use that in another tradition, well, they will just have to do that on their own, but it is not Feri. The Black Heart isn't some abstraction or some allegory. It is simple, primitive fact.

Possession
... from Victor

Could you give a definition of possession and what that truly is? A lot of people have different ideas about what it is, or the dangers of it, or what it means, more or less, in the Feri work. How would you define that?

Possession is two kinds. If your God Self, or in Vodou it is called *Maitre Tet*, gives permission for a spirit to work with you, and through you, then you go into a kind of sleep, and you take part in it. But you never give up your individuality. You're never conquered. You're never screwed over by something. You remain yourself. In Hawaiian we called it *noho*, which means "to sit." But it cannot happen if your God Self forbids it.

Now I'm going to give you three words right out of the language of the Feri people. The first word is *Vivi*, that would be what is called the *Unihipili* or Fetch. *Emi* is what has been called the Talking Self or *Uhane*. *Ori, L'Ori,* or *Eleda*, is the *Aumakua* or God Self. So you see, it's all over the world. We know what we are. If we know what we are, we can be freed. The truth can set us free.

The danger in possession is if you let alien beings in to use you—and there are plenty out there that will. They'll split your personality. They'll touch certain parts of your personality that you don't even know you have. And then, you won't be able to consciously remember when one takes over or when one doesn't, even though it's all you. That's the danger of possession. Another danger is that they can come in with cruel and terrible ideas and infect you with them. Because when someone knocks at your door, and I'm not just speaking about spirits, *don't let them in* unless you know who they are. You turn on the light first, and that light is right above your head. That is your Holy Ghost, your

Aumakua. Turn that on first. And then, you will be able to deal with possession.

Not possession in the sense of loss of self, but in the sense of working as a horse that willingly carries a higher intelligent being until it is time to part company. It is a loving relationship, not something horrible. Not something terrifying, although I've seen this happen. Unfortunately, in my work as a Vodou priest, I've noticed many people get possessed by spirits who claim to be something they are not. They claim to be Damballa or Shango or something, when actually they are beings we should not mess with. Not all spirits like that are evil. There's just some things that we simply would not mess with because they're not us. We don't stick our hand in a nest of snakes out in the desert, then go out and kill all the snakes if we survive. What we do, we have to be ourselves because the Gods respect and love us. Otherwise, don't ever worship a God that is not yours, and above all, be careful that your own Aumakua always is in full possession, which means self-possession, not displacement.

Salvation
... from Cora

Being saved is when the three selves of the individual are talking to each other, and he or she gets in touch with themselves. When you know you've done wrong, say you have mistreated someone, then you go to them with your three selves aligned and you speak about it, and say, "Now I won't do this anymore." And so you don't. Because your three selves won't let you. Being saved is what happens when you get in touch with your three selves, and know them, and get everything clean between them, and make things right with others. When you know your God Self. As Victor used to say, "May all three selves be straight within."

So the three selves guide you to act properly.

Yes.

And that's salvation, or being saved?

I think it is. Now that's your lesson for the day (*laughs*).

LETTERS TO STUDENTS

Written by Cora, March 20, 1996

Dear Student,

I'm very happy you are interested in Vodou. The very roots of our religion are in Africa. The way you write, it seems that you have a good grasp on the roots of the Craft. My advice would be to learn and practice the Ha Prayer and Kala Rite. The best way to do this is to take a glass of water and take four breaths and then exhale until you have done sixteen. Charge the water by placing your hands over the glass till you see it steaming. Then drink the charged water, feeling it going to every part of your body. You should feel light and clean. (See page 43 of my book.) If your partner wishes to study Kahuna, he should talk to Victor, as he is one of the last Kahuna and knows the subject well.

You are wise to stay out of the Witch wars. They accomplish nothing. I hesitate to recommend a teacher. There are so few that teach the real thing. Victor and I will be very glad to correspond with you.

Most Pagans use the word "eclectic" in a derogatory manner. There is nothing wrong with using the word if used correctly. It means to pick up information from various sources and use it. Most people in the Craft do this.

However, we can also learn from meditation and communing with the Gods.

We are especially interested in your background in folk magic and healing. Perhaps we can get together sometime and write a book. I grew up in Alabama and am also familiar with polecat grease. My grandfather was an herb doctor and was famous for his potions and folk remedies. Our tradition has its roots in Vodou, of course, but also Ireland.

I'm interested in your Bumblebee Method of card reading. This method of reading the playing cards is similar to the one Victor uses. The Gypsies taught him, and we haven't found anyone else that uses it.

Victor and I will be pleased to meet you. While you are here, call us and we can arrange a time for you to visit us.

I think this is all for now, but we can write more another time.

Blessed be,
Cora

Written by Cora, July 31, 1994

Dear Students,

Victor and I find your question about the male God interesting, and we'll help you clear up any confusion. When the Goddess conceived the dual Consort, she drew into herself two bright spirits, thus becoming the mother, sister, and lover in a way that is just as natural as a nucleus picking up two electrons in the cool darkness between the stars to become an atom of helium. And those two electrons form an aura or cloud about the nucleus to form what we call the "k-shell." The two parts of the Consort have the same kind of oneness we have in the two lower parts of the soul, but in the perfect love of the Godhead. When working as one, they become the oldest of all the male Gods, whom the Christians and some other religions tried to make into the Devil.

If you will read what I've said in my book* once more, after reading this part of my letter, the confusion will go away.

In the oldest form of the Craft, the Guardians were named for four interstellar Gods of the Nephilim. This word is the plural of *nephelon*. When you name the Guardians, what really happens is that four of the Holy Ones who are all about us come and join your working in the names of the ancient Gods we honor. There is not just one group of four of these spirits that act as Guardians. Wherever we are, four of the Holy Ones come and join our circle. The same Gods come and work with us whether we are Lakota shamans or what light-skinned people called Witches.

---

* See *Fifty Years in the Feri Tradition*, pp. 7–9.

In what we call the Feri tradition, there are secret names for the Guardians that have been remembered and handed down through the many generations, from the time when the Nephilim came to us before the Ice Age. At that time, they materialized in both male and female form and had sex with some of our distant ancestors and brought forth some of the first humans of the kind we now call Witches. Among Native American shamans, these God-people are referred to as one of the Star Nations. If you have any questions about this, we will be glad to discuss them.

The purpose of the Circle is to hold in the power and place us in between the worlds and shift our perception in the working. Here is a brief but beautiful example of casting a Circle:

The priestess stands at the north and the priest at the south. The priestess gives him the athame, blade pointed up. He then steps back, well within the Circle, and points the blade in all four directions, north to west clockwise. Beginning in the north he says, "By the earth that is her body"; the east, "By the air that is her breath"; to the south, "By fire that is her spirit"; and to the west, "By the water that is her womb." Facing the north again, he says, "Evo he, blessed be."

After the coven has tended to the business at hand, all link hands and say,

> Out of the air from everywhere.
> This work is formed before the dawn.
> Back into the air to everywhere,
> That which is done, may now be gone.

Then they all spend the rest of the evening having a good time.

Blessed be,
Cora

Written by Victor, [date unknown]

Dear Student,

You have been wanting to know the tools necessary to begin the practice of Vodou. The essential materials are not so hard to come by. The main trouble is in finding the right kind of drum and making the *asón*, our sacred rattle. I would say to start collecting herbs of all kinds. You never know until you get into the swing of it just what kind of powders, oils, and so on you are going to need. You will need gunpowder and sulfur, as well as cornmeal and flour, which are easy enough to buy. Practice drawing the *vévés* of the Gods as accurately as you can, in the different kinds of powders and colored chalks and varieties of soil.

Vodou is something that you sort of slide into like collecting the materials for ordinary Witchcraft. There are a lot of similarities between Pictish Witchcraft and Vodou, but this is not obvious to the non-initiated. I have an odd but familiar sensation when a black mambo or houngan tells me what I am doing, even when the symbols are different and the drums are not speaking. When I drew the swastika before a mambo I trusted, she said that is the sign of Ogou Zandor and Shango, as it was used in Tunei very long ago when the world was young. Witchcraft as I practice it blends in so well with Vodou that I see nothing derogatory in saying that the black people incorporated much of it into their rites through contact with racially white Witches. On the other hand, it is true that they really had it, so where they did borrow, it was more of a rediscovery of things that once existed at the very fountain of human mystical experience and inspiration. We who are partly Pictish, or almost purely so, have the firm belief that our ancestral home was Mother Africa. On a very deep level, there is a strong kinship with black people.

I am sure you already know enough to take the first steps in the Art. Words sometimes get us into a strange bind, and as almost everyone says "Voodoo," I think a good compromise is "Vodou," which is pronounced the same way. Watch the way I use the different spellings, as I may use the word "Voodoo" to emphasize the powers and the Loa of the Gods. The truth is that we will both be learning. I do not claim to know everything about Vodou, and have as great a need and desire to learn more as do you, even though I have lived close to black people all my life and am partly black myself on my father's side through the Spanish heritage.

If I were to wake up some morning and find myself blue-black with a head of fluffy hair, I would not feel my soul to be in an alien body. The best way to say it is that I am just me, and do my best to be understood by those I consider worthwhile as sisters and brothers. I know that when I hear the passionate, intricate rhythms of the drums speaking to Legba and Damballa, they are calling me back to my native world. I have incarnated in many lives and among several races, and I've learned a strange thing. The more free and, one might say, fluid you become as a spirit, the more adept you become at changing planes of expression and consciousness, and remain the real you in whatever modality you express in. This brings great rewards when the time comes to take up life on the spirit side of living. This opens up many otherwise inaccessible planes in the unseen world. In each form and mode of expression you are being real; otherwise, you could not even be aware of such planes, much less find them or stay on them for long. So the pipes could call me to the Isle of Skye, the cry of the Kahuna chants and the steel guitars to Hawai'i and so on, and each place would be part of the real me.

Here is an amazing thing that soul travel has taught me: no matter how different these modalities seem, they are all part of the same spectrum of being. It is only limitations,

mistranslated as ego, from which we must try and free ourselves. In doing this, we regain, not lose, the many colors
and modes of being. When we are free from the limitations
of a thing, we have in no sense overcome it. We have freed
it and made it more real, and then we find the limitations
have, in a sense, been an illusion from which the very modality of being has been trying to free itself.

For example, and I admit it is a pale one, if you are an
Irishman who can speak only with a brogue, and overcome
your limitations without losing your Irishness, you can go
back and be a real Irishman. Music and poetry prove this
very well. To be what we really are, we must overcome
the limitations. Then we are that and much more. We have
opened whole new worlds for worship without losing a
thing. It may seem strange of me to be saying these things,
but Vodou itself teaches them. The amazing truth is that
Damballa and Aida are the Ophidian forms of Krom and
Mari of the tiny dark aborigines of Scotland, Ireland, and
the ancient British Islands.

In black terms, Mawu is the great ancestral mother, the
Great Goddess of many names and forms. Her true sex was
changed only in patriarchal times, which are more recent
in origin than history will allow us to believe. She is both
male and female in one body. And Elizabeth Gould Davis
puts it so clearly in speaking of the most perfect and original human race. The Picts considered it gallant to speak
of Krom the mighty first, and it was not a male chauvinist
term of speech as some would think. But sometimes we say
the reverse, and speak of Mari first. This is to say that the
male always comes from the female.

In Vodou, Aida can conduct Damballa, or Damballa can conduct Aida like a circle of lightening. In Greek
terms, she can be Androphoros, or he can be Estrophoros.
Further in the deep, inner mysteries of Vodou, the Maitre Tet is the same as the Aumakua of Hawaiian Kahuna,
the third guardian angel or God Self, the third spirit of the

human soul. It is of dual sex, both female and male. The threads of the *gran misterre* run deep, connecting all ancient cultures from Africa where the human race began, through Polynesia, on through ancient matriarchal Greece to the Norse people.

How the heart of the initiate thrills when the antique mysteries are written of. She or he recognizes the same great truth expressing itself in many forms, yet as one thing. Nor should we bypass ancient India.

It is growing late, dear friend, and I must break off, though it is hard to leave the fire of inspiration even for rest. I will take up more when I hear from you, which I hope will be sooner than you have heard from me. Please pardon me for this. I have always remembered you to the Gods, and my own personal Loa, and mon Maitre Tet.

Blessed be,
Victor

Dictated by Victor, February 13, 1992

Dear Anaar,

I should tell you a little bit about myself. I was born in Clayton, New Mexico. I am mostly Irish and Spanish with some Native American, including Polynesian. The rest of my history is so complicated that I think I'll go into it more as we go along. I was strongly influenced as I was growing up by the strange racial mixture that I am. Especially by the Mexicano culture, the Mayan Indian, and the Apache that I am kin to, which is mixed with a little Choctaw as well, because of the way the tribes were shuffled around in the early days, quite a long time before I was born. And I remember my incarnation in Mexico and in Guatemala, as well as the life I lived in Hawai'i before I came into this incarnation.

The Craft, which we have called the Feri Tradition for quite a few years now, was handed down through the family, and in its Native American form through the Mexicano people that I grew up with, especially the Yaqui and the Papago and other kinds of Mexican Indian people that lived in Albuquerque and Clayton and places like that. I spent a lot of time in Albuquerque when I was a very young child.

When I was very young, I had an accident that deprived me of physical eyesight. For a few months, I was completely blind. But I developed etheric sight. I was always able to see clearly in my dreams, because we do leave the body when we sleep. And the spirits always woke me up outside of the body. They never allowed me to slip into the limitations of this present incarnation; the good things, yes, but not the limitations. I was never allowed to just go out and be a mere child in my dreams. That never occurred.

Blue Fire

The blue fire is a higher manifestation of what is called *chi*, what Hiroshima called chi in his beautiful book on the subject. I don't know where to get the book now, but he spoke of this energy that pervades all things, and spoke of the very, very fine particles, which in parts of India are called *mulaprakriti*. The blue fire is just one manifestation of that.

The blue fire is a higher form of energy and should be handled with care if it is drawn from the environment, and out of your own person, and your own body, and so forth. Like I said, it must be handled with care because it is more actinic; it's less organic than ordinary mana, as we call it in Hawaiian. Ordinary chi that exists in the warm flesh of the body is a little different than the stronger forms of it, but it is the same thing, just as the different colors of light are the same thing. It's all photons, it's all waves of light. I don't know why people say that blue fire is the only manifestation, because it's just a higher energy form of the chi force of nature, of which all things are made.

The Star Goddess

About the blue fire coming from the womb of the Star Goddess: Now as we know, Amaterasu is the Japanese word for the spirit within the sun, and also the great God Herself. We say "Goddess" because people have worshipped the Deity as a purely male and purely masculine being—based on a strange theory of theology—for so long that we have to differentiate sometimes. But when we say "Goddess" in my tradition, we mean God Herself, because God was first worshipped and first perceived by the ancient human beings as the Great Mother, although this Great Mother has the power that we think of as male.

44

Now long ago, I would say eighteen to twenty billion years ago—modern science has not yet decided—the big bang occurred. The universe began as a very small, tiny seed egg, which in ancient India was called *bindu*. The seed egg was in the womb of the natural mother of the universe. We do not think of God as a necessary theory to account for a first cause in creation. The creation was just as natural as the bringing forth of a child in your womb from a fertilized egg. Only in this case, the Blessed Virgin of the Outer Darkness did not have to have any help to bring it forth. It came from her naturally because she was the natural mother, the natural extension of the universal creation, just as you are the natural extension of nature when you bring forth a child.

Her companion, the God, is brought forth from her because the male is mutated out from the female. Actually, there are two of these spirits with her at all times. But we speak of either one of them as the God, because they are exactly alike, identical spirit twins, the bright dual Consort of the Blessed Mother. In her are all the powers and potencies of nature.

You will probably remember the Shinto Goddess who looked at herself in her mirror. Her companion is a God of storms and power. It's very similar to our own way, to the Feri way. Susano'o creates thunderstorms and is somewhat feared by the older people. They were sort of afraid of him, but he was considered like we consider the Horned God, a lord of fertility and power. In short, the Lord. As they say in Spanish, *El Señor*.

I remember seeing a picture years ago in which one of the shogun was depicted with a horned helmet. Now the sign of the horns is very predominant all over the world in different cultures, not so much in the Polynesian, but in other places, especially among the American Indians. Our Native Americans, the Oglala Sioux, speak of the Great Mother as Great White Buffalo Woman or Great White

Buffalo Calf Woman. Sometimes just White Buffalo. And she is the nearest thing to an individual supreme being.

The rest, the Universal, the Kami that is in everything, is referred to by the Indians as Wakan Tanka, which means "magic mystery" or "holy mystery." In Mexico, there is a city that is called Teotihuacán, meaning "the Gods who dwell in the magic place." Sometimes it's interpreted as "violent place of the Gods," but that's not really a correct definition, because *teo* means "the Gods," and *ti huacán* means "who dwell in the magic mystery." So the Gods are great spirits of nature, not patriarchal dictators.

The Points of the Pentagrams

The Iron Pentagram is sex, self, passion, pride, power. The Pentagram of Pearl is love, wisdom, knowledge, law, power. They are both equally sexual. There is no dichotomy between sex and love in the mother religion as there is in the patriarchal faiths. Male-dominated religion started out with a pretense of pro-sexuality, but ended up with celibate priesthoods, sadomasochistic practices, mortification of the flesh, and all that travesty, which is complete *bakutari* nonsense.

The Blue God

The Blue God is what we might refer to as the most heavenly form of God—that is to say, the spirit plane farthest out from what we call the physical—the closest being or pair to the Great Goddess herself. Now in ancient India, Parvati is the White Goddess. Kali is the same Goddess, only in her dark, potent form as the power of darkness in the womb of light. She brought forth the God not because she had to have someone to help her as a creatrix, but out of divine lust. She wanted him, and out of her passion she brought him forth.

46

Their act of love, which is the act of creation, is the same love that we have. When we have sex, we are simply echoing that which occurred eighteen to twenty billion years ago, when the universe, or at least a big section of it, was born out of the primordial fireball. So we are the stuff that the stars are made of. The Blue God is not a separate God from, say, Thor or Limba.* Limba is an African term. Thor is not, of course, that's Scandinavian.

Arddhu

Arddhu is the dark form of the God. Just as the Holy Mother has her dark form, so the God has his, which is Arddhu in Welsh. In Haiti he is called Papa L'inglesou; and in Japan, Suza.

Nimue

Now there's been a lot of misunderstanding about the identity of Nimue, Mari, and Anna. Nimue is like a very small human child. When we see a human child, female, of about five or six years, especially among the light-skinned peoples, and I can say truthfully also certain of the Oriental, we see something of this phase of the personality of God Herself. She has three phases in which she operates, and they appear among we human beings here on this planet in different stages of our life. But they always exist in the Mother, just as all the colors exist in the sun, in the sunlight. So, what expresses itself in our young females is Nimue.

---

* Many Feris also spell his name "Lemba."

Mari

Mari is the full bride of heaven, the full moon, the moon that fills all desire and fills all heaven with pure flame. This is Mari. Mari is an old Feri word which means "mother of water." Mari. And is the same as Miriam, Mariana, and Mariko.

Now this Great Mother as I said, being God Herself, is both male and female in one, but is feminine, a feminine being, and bisexual. However, as I have said before, there are many of the Gods of nature who are similar to the powers of the Mother because they are Mother's children. We are all Mother's children.

The universe is not empty. The oldest of all religions is polytheistic, not monotheistic. Why should there be just one Father-Mother in an empty house? No way. The universe should be, and is, teeming with life. Even the stars are homes of Gods. We know this. That is why people like myself, who have the mixture that I have, pay homage to the great sun, because Father-Mother Sun is a living thing, a living creature.

And by the way, sun is not just Father. Planets come out of her. So we sometimes celebrate the male power that emanates from the sun, and sometimes the female power. So Oaha'atuihine is one form of the Mother-Sun. And Teramatu Atame also is the same as the Ra Inte of the South American Indians or the Ra of Egypt. And the other I mentioned is the same as Amaterasu.

One interesting thing about that name is that regardless of any linguistic connections, if we analyze the word, again we have *ama*, which is "mother," *te ra*, "the sun," and *su*, "magic, light." Amaterasu, the primordial sun from which all things came forth. The great fireball out of which all other things, all the stars and everything, were condensed when it expanded and formed itself into great clouds. Very fascinating, because even modern physics bears this out.

Now I would like to point out that in the Feri Tradition, as I was brought into it, and has existed since the human race walked out of Africa, the idea of Red Mari and Blue Mari—well that is not really of the Feri Faith. If that is just someone's poetic inspiration, then that's his way. And if he wants to do this, let it be his tradition. It could be part of a lovely poem, or a song, if one wanted to give a special inspirational song like that to a Red Mari. So there's nothing wrong with that, I mean I'm not quarreling with it. I'm just saying that it isn't in the rituals of the Feri Faith as I know it. But if someone has a beautiful song of that kind, and likes to praise the Goddess in that way, then that's fine, that's all right.

Mari is the White Goddess in the Feri Tradition. White in the sense that the sun is white, not racist, but white in the sense of a white flower, the pure light. We also speak of the Goddess as Kali when we say,

> Hail, Blessed Mother,
>> whose body is light
>> and whose voice is truth.
> Power of darkness
>> and womb of light.

And we know in physics that the blacker the body, the brighter will be the light when it's heated to incandescence. So black is power. So is white, but white is radiant power, giving out, going out like positive chi. Black receives, and can be cold, but is also, in its way, positive. Black is the womb, and white is like the phallus. But that does not mean that light is male and dark is female. Of course, there can be male light, and female dark. But then people have a tendency to grab onto these things and make a dogma out of them.

There are some people who argue with me that the God, because he was called Lucifer at one time, God of light, that he's supposed to be God of light and warmth and every-thing, and that's his province, and that darkness and the cold and everything—that's poor Hecate or Diana or some-thing like that, and she's left out in the dark. I think that's rather foolish.

It's just like yin-yang. Yin-yang can express itself in many ways. Yin-yang can express itself in a woman as well as in a man. Or, as man and woman, or as woman and man. But it is what it is. So I believe we have in the yin-yang principle, the same thing, almost exactly, as positive-negative in electricity. But not quite as polarized, not quite as definite.

We know chi, or *qi*, can vibrate back and forth, as well as flow in several directions at once, which often is done when we follow the way of *kami no michi*.* We realize that we begin, all of us begin, as feminine beings. So the male, despite all his vaunted pride and wanting to rule the world and so forth, is in a sense an imperfect woman. So what are we going to do with that? I say in answer to that, so what? Enjoy it.

Anna

Returning to the Goddess, Anna is the same energy as Kali. But the Black Goddess is not a separate Goddess. Nimue, Mari, and Anna are not three separate Goddesses. They are one Goddess, one God. They are God Herself—the three phases of God Herself, just as the moon has three phases. There aren't three moons, but three phases.

If you read my poetry, I wrote one about the Pictish priestess, and that tells quite a lot about the old way among the small people and how they worshipped God. It was not a patriarchal form of monotheism, as I've just tried to point out, but a very natural way of looking at things.

---

* The way of the Gods

The Triune Soul

You asked a question about the God—that is what we call in the Jewish language the Elohim, the divine parents—being related to the three selves. The only way I can answer that is to tell you what the three selves in the human being really are. And again, this is rather complicated. But we will be patient, I hope, and go through it as we go along.

I'll begin by approaching it from the Hawaiian way. We have three words for the soul in the Hawaiian language: *Unihipili*, *Uhane*, and *Aumakua*. Now, *Unihipili* means "the sticky one." Uhane refers to either the whole soul or the middle part. And *Aumakua* means "the eye" or "self-parents," both male and female. It is the third and highest of our three spirits.

Now in the Jewish language, the two lower parts are called *Nephesh* and *Ruach*. *Ruach* means something like "divine wind." Again, we have one of the oldest forms of *kamikaze*. And this divine wind of life is associated with what is sometimes called the "Middle Self," because it has more reasoning power, and can direct like the sails of a ship, and can use the wind more. Whereas, Nephesh is more impulsive; it's more our animal self, the rough soul.

Then we have the speaking and thinking self, which is spoken of as Uhane in this particular context. Then we have the Aumakua, which is the same as the Kami Self, the Star, the Buddha soul. This dwells at the top of the aura. And just as we have different parts of the brain, like the right and left side of the physical brain, so we have the two lower parts of the soul. The Unihipili and the Uhane, or the Nephesh and Ruach.

The body of Nephesh is that part of you that contains what science calls the subconscious mind. It is shaped like your physical body, but not exactly. It extends out from your physical body on all sides for about two centimeters. The Ruach body is your true aura, and is oval- or egg-shaped but follows the outer part of the human body, as long as your soul surrounds and interpenetrates the human body. Because the soul is not in the human body, but around it; it surrounds the human body. Otherwise we wouldn't know much more about what is inside ourselves.

In the ancient language of the Feri religion, as we call it now, there are three words for the parts of the soul: *Vivi*, which means the same thing as the Unihipili, or Nephesh; *Emi*, which is the same thing as the Ruach soul, or Uhane; and *Ori*, which is the same as the God Self or Aumakua. And when we speak in the English, we say that we are made of the Animal Self, the Human Self, and the God Self. There is nothing derogatory or pejorative about the word "animal." Patriarchal religion has blunted the sensitivity of much of the world's perception of the nature of the human life, and made us ashamed of where we came from, denying evolution, etc.

Now I'll give you a little bit about the appearance of these three parts. The body of the Vivi—and read this carefully, so you won't get mixed up in the words—the body of the Vivi is usually sort of a silvery blue-gray color when you first see it, but as you look at it carefully, and your spirit sight, what we call etheric sight, opens more, you see that it glows with a beautiful pink color as well, a kind of electric pink. As I said, it extends about two centimeters out from the flesh on all sides. This vital, etheric body double contains an awful lot of substance. And as will be apparent later, when you travel outside of your body, you only take a very small amount of astral matter to form the vehicle that you travel in. Most of the vital body stays behind.

So if you learn how to travel outside of your body, then you have used part of this vehicle, and you have been conscious in all three parts. You've probably heard the expression, part of a prayer, "Let all three souls be straight within me." That's what it means. Everything's aligned, with no complexes in between to bar the way to the God Self.

So that is what the three selves are like. Now, of course, nature has the three great powers, all over the place; everything we see is in threes. And we have, like in the *Star Wars* stories about the Force, the dark side and the bright side. And then we have that third power that orders things and reasons things and manifests itself in consciousness. In other words, consciousness is like the very shape of the universe. And we can't say that anything in the universe is not conscious. My sensei taught me a word for that, she said it was called *kami-no*.

And we are then taught that we are personifications of nature. The Gods are real persons, not just figures to help us understand the powers of nature, because if that were true, we wouldn't be here. I've had people say Gods are just archetypes. Well, we're archetypes, but we are still living, thinking beings.

The Secrets of the Craft

Anything I can tell you, I would be glad to share with you, because the secrets of the Craft are like the secrets of science. How in the world can you learn if you don't ask, if you don't try to learn? Everybody has a right to know how they are made and how these things work. It's just that the people who belong to the Craft, if they're really following the right way, are like scientists or doctors. And they should have the responsibility and the dignity of all of that. But the knowledge shouldn't be withheld from people, and we shouldn't say, "We're the only ones who have a right for it." Everyone has a right to know.

But can everyone handle it? Can everyone know? Can everyone be a doctor or a musician? No. It's a religion that comes from the very heart of what is called the common people. It's a religion of the soil, it's comes out of primitive human beginnings. It's primitive human sorcery, religion, emotion, feelings. It is a very sexual, a very occult, a very powerful and, in the case of the Feri Tradition, a very martial Art.

I do hope that in reading what I have just said, you will catch a glimpse of that wonderful light of self-realization. We come to have the revelation of the clear light, to learn that we are part of the universe. You are part of the Universal, what Master Hiroshima called the Universal. You are part of that. And as that, there is Kami in you and in everything else. So you come to your true place and realize yourself as a woman, a person.

You don't have to try to figure out what you're here for, that will come later. The idea is to attain your self-awareness, your consciousness, what is sometimes called the "no mind," though that doesn't mean "not mind." It's not a negative sense of the word. I believe you will know what I'm speaking of. But it is the state of realization, like the haiku that I wrote, which says:

> My thoughts are petals,
> Floating on the serene lake
> Of inner selfhood.

Find that apparently timeless state of being in which you are you. You are a person. And you come to realize this. And when you do, you will realize that whether you were born again as a man or woman, you'd still be you, no matter what name you have, or what race you belong to in another life, or another circle. You are a spirit with a body, as well as a body with a spirit, because it's all the same. All matter and energy are the same. $E=mc^2$.

That is one reason why there is a mirror on my altar, to symbolize the clear light. I don't look in the mirror, and I don't let other people look in it unless it's absolutely necessary. I take it outside and reflect the sun and moon in it. And when the sky is very beautiful, I take it outside as an act of devotion to nature and to the Gods, and then I bring it back in and I place it on the altar where I honor the Gods and my ancestors.

Poppets and Paper Boats

Now, speaking of making poppets for rain, in ancient times we also made little, tiny clay statues representing rain Gods and spirits and so forth, and set them out on stones out in the woods to pray for different things, like rain and sun. And the precious lady I told you about, my teacher, showed me how to make little paper boats with tiny candles in them and put them out on the water, like in a creek or, well not exactly a river, because that's too much current, but say a swift running stream. And you put the paper boat in after you light the candle. You put them on there after you make your prayer, and the boat goes away. And that's one of the ways of making a prayer.

She also made for me a little paper prayer wheel that you set in water. She waxed the paper so that it wouldn't get soggy in the water. And then she put tiny bits of camphor on little metal pieces, and when she put the wheel down on the surface of water, if the water was still, it would turn and turn for the longest time, until the camphor finally dissolved. She would also put little bits of camphor gum on the bottom of the tiny paper boats, and put those in the water, and they would propel themselves. It really was a marvelous thing to watch.

The Path of the Heart

I have read Starhawk's book,* and I can't agree with everything she says, but I pick out what I can. Like I have said to you before, if people want to have different ideas in their traditions, then that is their path. One must always follow

* *The Spiral Dance*

the path of their heart. That is very necessary. You cannot follow a path that you don't belong in. You have to find some version of it, or some right path. Always the path of your heart is what you must follow.

So it is with the Craft. We can't afford to say we agree with everything in it. You're going to find a lot of ideas that will be rather strange to you. I know I find ideas that are strange to me. Like that Red and Blue Mari ... it's pretty, and if a person wishes to adore the Gods in that way, like I said before, that's fine, but I can't say that it is a part of Feri ritual. Because Feri ritual is more kin to the African ways, as I have said before. And then next to that, it is kin to certain of the Oriental ways.

And I have found, in my affinity with the Japanese people, quite a lot of similarity. There's a deep psychic bond between us, and I find that they understand a good deal of what I know. And in some instances, in fact in quite a few instances, I can't communicate to the average Caucasian the same thing that I can to the Japanese-American person who is more oriented toward the magic and religion of Japan. And then the Hawaiian guys, you know (*laughs*)—I knew quite a lot of those, and being part Hawaiian myself, I have quite a lot of affinity with them, too. So whether they talk to me in cultured English or *da kine*, or whatever, we have more of an understanding of what we're talking about.

Then, of course, the Mexicanos—I find a lot of understanding among them, even though they are quite Catholic. There are things in the Catholic faith that I understand and things I disagree with. But I'm too much Spanish and Irish to think of the Catholic religion as alien. Although again, a lot things in the Catholic religion I can't agree with (*laughs*). But I don't like what most people call Protestant either. It's sort of ... too male; there's no Virgin Mary or anything like that in it, and I just don't care for religion like that. No saints, nothing like that. Because the saints, really, are old Gods changed over to join the church (*laughs*). That's what most of them are.

Woman's Power

The Craft is not a religion where you become selfless, or you become humble in that way that allowed people to once say, "I'm not doing the work, but the Lord is doing it." You do want the power. You are a woman. Witchcraft is woman's right. Her natural place is to have this power. You are *miko*, whatever else you might be. So you have a right to want to possess this power because you are the power. The light comes from within you as well as without. You do not have to bow your head to the Gods in submission. You might with love and reverence. But not in the way that the Christians and some sects of Buddhism do, to the purely male hierarchy of Gods, or one male God.

Witchcraft is not a patriarchal religion. The male is honored in Witchcraft, but the male is male in the purely sexual sense, not a dominant, domineering sense. Because the Craft, the real Craft, honors woman in her true place. She is mother, lover, the very beginning of our life. We have all been man and woman at one time. I guess that some people have lived several lives in one sex, but I have never met one that did too many. I know I have been man and woman through the lives that I can remember. In ancient Greece, I was a woman and a man, and I have other memories like that. And in Britain—that was the life I mentioned where I remembered having a child—I was a Druidess. And among the small people of Britain before the Romans came, and that's quite awhile ago.

But anyway, remember the Pentagram: sex, self, passion, pride, power. There is a rich and lovely part of Japanese heritage that speaks of honor and self-discipline, which is not just self-control, but self-discipline. To walk the true way, to follow the *getsumei no michi*, whether you call it Craft or not, you follow this. You find the moonlit path within you; you find the way of the sunlight on the water; you learn how to let the wind blow the water until there are waves all over the lake of your being. And then how to still the water, so that the sun may express and reflect until you can see the inverted Tree of Life and the sun of Divinity in the still water of your conscious being.

Come to know that you are, regardless of time or space, you are. And you are part of the universe, you are a molecule of the Universal. And your atoms of that molecule are the three parts of your soul. Just as a molecule of water in the ocean contains one atom of oxygen and two of hydrogen. And you are of the sea; you are of the sea of life and consciousness; you are a part of Kami; you are a part of life. You are you.

A wise man once said to me, although it has been said before a lot of times as a rather frivolous joke, "Do you know how to spell 'guru?'" And I said, "G-u-r-u. Gee, you are you!" And we both laughed. He said, "Now that is the thing to remember." Any religion that tries to take your self—or your will, your ego, your determination—away from you, do not follow it, because it leads only to disillusionment. Then he lifted his hand very reverently and blessed me in the name of Vacnani, which is the name of the Goddess in the Indian language. And he was a wonderful guy. He lived a perfectly normal life with a wife and children, and he was very wise and very learned.

So we who follow the Craft, by whatever name it is called, should be very natural in everything we do. Live a normal, wholesome life. Whatever we do, it is because God Herself needs to do it. When we make love, God needs to make love. When we eat, God needs to eat. We breathe, God needs to breath. And we have a saying in my tradition of the Craft, which is a little tough to wrap yourself around, but it's a very good saying: God is self, and self is God, and God is a person like myself.

Power and the Pentagrams

Now let's have a few more words about power here while I'm thinking about it. Most people think of power as power over something. There are people—especially men—who want power over their wives, power over their political party, power over a country, power over a gun, or a dog, or something like that. And I think they would rather kill than make love. I think they don't know how to make love, they make hate. And it's always the thing about the rough soul gone wild, you know?

Power is like the sun. The sun has power. A healthy body has power. If you have power, good health, vitality, strength in all of your being, that is power. The power to do things—just like you have the power to cook your meal, or play music, or walk, or ride a bicycle, or drive a car—this is power. When people say power corrupts, they mean domination of other people. When a person uses power in the wrong way, they don't really have that power. If everyone turns against such a person—like Hitler, for example—the person is revealed as nothing, absolutely nothing, because they are not power.

You must become power yourself. Then say, "I am power. I don't just have power, I am power." Sex, self, passion, pride, and power. That's the Iron Pentagram. And remember that the Pearl Pentagram is not just a milder form, but a more thoughtful form. We've talked about the two great powers: the rough soul and the reasoning soul. They must work together—the dark side of the force and the bright side. But they are not two opposing things.

Darkness is not evil, light good, or the other way around either. That's a patriarchal idea. Like all male-dominated religion, it has its roots in the wrong kind of egotism. Now the word "ego" is from the Greek εγώ, which means simply "I am" or "I exist." So we are a religion of self and power, and lust in the sense that lust means powerful desire. Not like the wish to do somebody injury or anything like that, or to go out and sniff cocaine. That's not what I'm talking about. I'm just talking about the rich power of life itself, like the rushing wind, or the rain of the elements. And all these things are your right as woman because you are the hope of the human race. You are the gateway of life. You are the joy and the mystery of nature.

And when you realize this, when you know this within yourself, and lift up your head and say, "I am woman, I am me. I am the beginning and the end," then you will understand how to use the Pentagram of Iron and the Pentagram of Pearl.

There are other stars we use. There's the enneagram. The decagram, too, which is an expanded form of the enneagram.

If people don't care for each other, they are not going to use power wisely. You can have lots of abilities and powers, but if you lack the harmony, if your mana is out of tune with everything else, then you're like a wild horse jumping fences.

But you can't blame the power. It's the incompleteness that is within you that is the fault. Evil cannot exist unless something is left out, destroyed, or broken. So we have the enneagram, the nine points, which are sex, self, passion, pride, love, wisdom, knowledge, law, and power. To make the ten points, we add liberty; because we are liberated when we have, not self-control, but self-discipline. There is a difference.

The Story of the Ninja Warrior

I remember a story from part of the discipline that I follow, which is called *Kokoro*, meaning "at the heart of things." The story is that a ninja warrior was confronted with a brother who was as evil as a man could possibly be, and yet still have power, still have physical abilities. He was an expert in the martial arts, they both were. He realized that there was no way to keep his family from being raped and murdered and eaten by this evil ninja, except to kill him, or be killed in the effort.

Well, he went to the shrines and he prayed. He asked the Kami to help him. The ancestors told him, "Go on and do what you have to do. You have *giri* to do this, you must do it!" So he went out. Now we know that the ninja did not always dress in black, but in the story, he dressed all in black, and he put on black mask and black gloves and took no weapons with him. He met the evil man and killed him, broke every bone in his body.

Then he went back to his home, and took off his black garments and put on a white kimono and went to the temple. Two men met him there. One had on a yellow robe and carried in his hands an empty brass bowl. The other man was dressed all in the black, that is the ritual garb of ninjutsu, so it's not necessarily what they wear all the time. But anyway, he was in the dojo part of the temple, where they practice the martial arts.

The man in the yellow robe came to the warrior, whose name was Hiroki, and he said, "Are you sorry that you killed a man? Do you not regret that you took a human life?"

The warrior bowed his head, and he said, "I am filled with sorrow that I have killed a man."

But the man in black walked up to him, and he said, "Samurai, are you sorry that you killed this evil man?"

And he answered, "No! I would do it again, with glory in my soul! At the thought of what he tried to do, fury rises in my heart."

And both men said to the warrior, "You have done well. Go now and pray for the soul of this man." So he did. And that is part of the understanding of what we call Kokoro, to truly come to know oneself, not as something aside from oneself, but as oneself. To know the Universal, and to know yourself as part of it, that is the thing that we all strive for. So that we can vibrate the membrane of Kokoro, and not create chaos, but keep on the path, and know ourselves as we are known. Within ourselves, within and without, round about, without doubt.

Witchcraft

"Witchcraft" is formed of two words. Witch is derived from *wicca* or *vitka*, which refers to wisdom and the Craft, the way to do things. In much the same way in old Hawai'i, Kahuna meant, "the secret," how to do things, and the secrets that must be kept. The wind blows on your face, and the sun shines upon you, and you are part of the wind and the sun. Part of the earth that is her body, the water that is her womb, the air that is her breath, and the fire that is her spirit. You are part of our Blessed Mother's creation, in fellowship and oneness with the Gods. And we are part of the Gods, and the Gods are part of us. We need them, and they need us.

So I must conclude this, and say, Evohe, Blessed be. Evohe is a word, by the way, which means, "Praised be the Lord," or the God. Evoe, without the *h*, refers to the Mother, the Goddess.

Blessed be,
Victor

Dictated by Victor, April 18, 1992

Dear Anaar,

You mentioned the martial arts aspect of the Feri Tradition. I can answer with an example. Not long ago, someone called an astrologer whom I know. And this lady proceeds to tell her a lot of garbage in answer to her question. The idea was her husband was getting out with another woman and was depriving her and doing all kinds of rotten things to her. So she asked the astrologer what to do.

Well, the astrologer proceeded to tell her all kinds of stuff about which planets were squared, and what astrological influences were impinging upon her. So when she asked, "What must I do about this situation?" the astrologer said, "Harmonize with your loved ones, and try to understand your husband better," and gave her some more stuff about her astrological sign, and his, and how "you must grow with each other," and on and on like that.

Now that is not martial. If the lady had come to me, I would have worked some spells to make this guy straighten up and fly right, and lure him into being attracted to his wife and have desire toward her. I would have given her things to do, to settle this stuff, and to win him back. Now that's one thing I mean by "martial." Another thing I mean is that if someone is trying to hurt you, you have a right to defend yourself.

A Christian preacher one time tried to do what the Pentecostal Church calls "praying you under convictions," so that I would "give way to the Lord," as he called it, and realize I was going to hell and worshipping demons and all that garbage. So I told him to stop his praying, because his praying was hurting me. That is energy, and there are natural laws that say if you hit somebody, it's going to hurt.

And there's no use getting some mental attitude about it. If somebody hits you with a rock, they hit you with a rock, it's going to hurt. If you learn how to defend yourself, and deflect the rock, that's fine. Well the same applies with magic.

So, I said, "All right, if you pray for me, I'll pray for you." Well in about seventy-two hours, he was screaming for mercy; he didn't want to be prayed for anymore. That's what I mean by martial. Because when his feet started going to sleep, and he began to get where he couldn't get up, or couldn't walk straight, he began to understand something was happening. There was something wrong! And the more he prayed, the worse it would get. So he agreed to quit. I told him, "All right, pack up your stuff, take your wife and kids, and leave the state." That's martial.

Now the point is that if he had kept it up, I would have stopped at a certain place, because I know how to defend myself. But there are valid reasons why I should have frightened him the way that I did. Because he was hurting the other members of his congregation through his prudery and through his tyrannical way of dealing with the people, just like Jimmy Swaggart and Jimmy and Tammy Bakker and all those kind of people do. That's the kind of preacher he was. So I scared the heck out of him, and he stopped messing with me. And he went back to his wife, and he started being more merciful with his congregation and not so much of a big hypocrite. It wasn't long after that, that he decided that he would leave the state, so he did, and I've not heard from him since. But I imagine that he has a good deal of second thoughts about praying somebody "under conviction" as he calls it, without their consent. No one has a right to do that. I would not do it. Not even if I was a Christian preacher, I would not do it.

One of my Witches whom I have trained for years was being hassled by a male chauvinist pig who wanted more than to just seduce, he wanted to commit rape on her and that kind of thing. He was absolutely evil. As they say, he was *un mal hombre*, a bad person, a bad man. So I decided that I would protect her, but I asked her permission. I didn't do it without her permission. I asked permission. She asked me questions, and because I'd been training her so long, we had this long conversation, and I agreed to allow her to use the magic to defend herself, which is the best thing.

So one night, this evil man was lying in his bed awake, and no doubt thinking some very raunchy thoughts about everybody in general, and her in particular, when he saw a glow of light in his room. And he looked, and he saw a perfect image of her completely naked, transparent, and glowing with a kind of greenish, white light. And her eyes were red when she looked at him. Well, she told him in some very raunchy language to let her alone or else. Then she floated over to him real quick and bit him. And that man screamed so loud that everybody in the apartments woke up, and they called the police. And he did have a bite, right on his neck.

Well the man let her alone ever since. That is another example of what I mean by the Feri Tradition of the Craft being martial, because it is, just like aikido when it's used for self defense. That is the way it is, because it is one of the oldest forms of magic known to the human race. The Witch I told you about just now actually had left her physical body and gone through the closed door of the man's apartment and then manifested herself and did the things I told you about.

The results would have been really terrible if he had not let her alone. As it was, ever after that, every time he would see her, he would get on the other side of the street— the sidewalk between the parts of the apartment. He would get on the other side of her, and he never spoke to her again, which is a very good thing. He never believed any of those things until then. Now he's a firm believer in the powers of black magic.

Now, you were asking about the difference between the warrior aspect of the Craft and the martial. Really, it's not different. It's just the way you behave yourself. The more you learn about these things that I've been discussing, the less likely you are to misuse them. Now, we know these things if we study the martial arts of Japan. We know that this is true. It's true of aikido and even ninjutsu. If you learn how to use these things, you learn so much while you're doing it that the abuse of these powers doesn't have any attraction for you anymore.

It doesn't mean that you won't use the power if you have to. But there are so many ways of using this knowledge in what some people would call a non-martial aspect. If you think about it, the medical possibilities are marvelous. Every power that we use can be used either to heal or in a martial sense. We can defend ourselves with the same power that we use to heal with. This is literally true. It's not just philosophy. It's not just a theory. It is fact, because the type of magic that we are talking about, the type of magic that I'm telling you about, is real.

The Black Goddess

Black has been the color associated with the Goddess as Kali. In one of the languages of ancient India, Kali means "the black one," and it has other meanings as well. And we have the black aspect of the Goddess as Cailleach in old Scotland. And Anna among the small people and the other Pictish tribes, and her sign was the waning moon. And we have the numerous Black Virgins in Christianity. And among the Gypsies, Sara Kali, who is really the Goddess Kali united with Virgin Mary, is quite black. There's a lot of power connected with the Black Virgins.

Throughout Eastern Europe, we notice this especially, and as I said among the Gypsies who consider that the Virgin Mary was possibly a manifestation of the same ancient Goddess who simply materialized, and gave birth to her son, and disappeared. That is a Gypsy belief, and I have found the same belief among the poorest Irish people. The so-called shanty Irish, the very poor Irish people, have the same belief. When St. Patrick came to Ireland, he had that belief, too. Moira, or Mary, which is sometimes spell M-E-R-I, was also the same person, and brought this last sacred king to birth.

The ancient Druids said that night is older than day, and darkness is older than light. We of the Feri Tradition have exactly the same teaching, which is in accord with modern physics. If you study cosmology, you will understand what that really means. And when you go beyond the atmosphere, out of body, which is in one way, quite safe, it doesn't have any untoward effect on the astral body, but for reasons I will explain later on, it is dangerous actually. So be careful of it. But when you go out on the edge of the atmosphere, the sky turns black. And again we find that same color.

The White Goddess

This white is not necessarily a "race" white, it's white like the moon. In Africa, she is called Kavia, and she's the same as the Moon Goddess all over the world. In Mexico, she's the same as Tonantzin, ancestress of all Gods, including such powerful Deities as Quetzelcoatl, Huitzilopochtli, and Yaumchuk the rain God. All Gods are really her children. Whether these Gods are feminine or masculine, they impinge upon our consciousness and work with us. We are all her children because she is the Mother of all.

White is her color the world over. Not the only color. There are usually three colors. Either red, white, and blue, or red, white, and black. The American flag, strangely enough, is one of the most appropriate symbols of our Lady that I can think of, even to the thirteen stripes and the fifty stars of the blue field. The three colors of her triple will. You would be surprised at all the different nationalities that mention her and give her much the same praise and much the same attributes all over the world. They all honor her as the great White Goddess of the moon and, actually, the universe—the Goddess of the entire universe—and the moon is her stone of power in reference to this planet when it circles it.

As you know, the woman is powerfully under the influence of her light, and the moon has within her a spirit of her own. All planetary bodies are homes of Gods. So are stars. Now, you know that in Japan, some of the girls, the geisha of today, and some of the Kabuki dancers painted their faces white. Well this whiteness is known, as I said, among all races. In the Native American ingredient of my own heritage, the Indians painted themselves white under certain conditions, the women that is. When the Apache woman had her first menstruation, she was called "The White Lady" and "The White Queen." And she was chalked white. And the young men came, and she laid her hands on them and blessed them. That was on the first night of her period.

The eclipse of the sun was associated with the darkness of the womb, and the eclipse of the moon was called the menstrual period of the Goddess, the menstrual blood of the White Goddess. In South America and in Mexico, in Yucatan and Guatemala, and all those places, Tonantzin and la Virgin Maria, as in the Virgin de Guadalupe, are in a sense the same person. This does not deny the existence of the mother of Jesus Christos any more than any other woman, because all women manifest the great one and are beings in their own right.

We are all her children, and you are being made aware as a woman of your natural divinity. Woman was really the first to be made in the image of God Herself, because the male is mutated from the female. Those who wrote the

Christian Bible said that a rib of Adam was used to make Eve, but they got it backwards. It's a hideous travesty on the mystery of birth. All human beings start out as female. Even as souls we are feminine, and all fetuses are female. And it takes a little shot of hormones to start them off as males. We are males in some lives, and in other lives we are females, but we all begin as female beings.

Colors and Symbols

Now, about color. I will have to be a little bit brief now, but I do want us to go into it. I have quite a lot of material on that gathered from my own experience and from my tradition about the meanings of color.

But we should clear one thing up. Color is not a mere allegorical symbol. You don't get together with a bunch of people and decide, "We're going to use green to represent frogs, and purple to represent sunsets," and so on. It has got to be what the energy really says to you. And we'll speak about the spiritual. One thing the Feri Tradition says is that spiritual is the quality of a creature or a thing. Physical is the state of matter and energy in which it exists and manifests. So we don't dichotomize between the mundane and the spiritual, or the physical and the spiritual.

All matter and energy are one thing. $E=mc^2$ is a good way to put it. Now, when we understand the way we react to color, and then decide how to use it, we're taking advantage of real knowledge. For example, red is associated with sexuality, courage, power, vitality, blood, danger, fury, and war, but also the most joyous and wonderful things that have vitality and energy. The human aura is a wonderful thing, and those colors in the human aura are marvelous to look at.

Black is a color. I know it's considered to be the absence of color, but that's only one kind of black. Black as a color is the twin of blue. Now that's hard to understand, but if you have out-of-body experiences, you will learn to perceive black as a color. Here, we do more than we realize, because when you put on a beautiful black dress, or you see a pretty black piece of cloth, it's beauty is due not only to the residual light, because we don't just make something that's *completely* absorbent, but also there is a color there, and we do perceive it. We understand it as a color.

We all feel the colors when we look at them, just like when you hear a note of music. A beautiful singer can sing an aria from an opera and hit a high note and just thrill us with its glory and its beauty. But you could also hear a terrible scream in the same key. It's the same way when you look at the colors of the human aura; in fact, any colors. And we react naturally to what the colors are, because what the colors mean really has its roots in what they actually are, as light and as energy that acts upon us.

We are simply glows of energy with physical bodies. We're the stuff the stars are made of. So, in a very real sense, light is truth, and truth is light. When we see the color orange in the human aura, we associate it with pride, a clean form of pride, like when a Flamenco dancer is dancing. And some kinds of Spanish Gypsy music can cause the colors orange and red and yellow to appear in the auras of the dancers. And yellow, the joyous wonderful color; and green, the color of healing; and blue, that shade of blue that is called indigo; and violet—all of these things are not just symbols that somebody has decided mean something.

They are the actual energies, the way we perceive these actual energies. And chromotherapy, which is a form of treatment with color, proves that this is true. Because people who are not even educated as to the so-called meaning, or the decided meaning, or arbitrary meaning, or allegorical meaning, react to the colors in the same way. So that's why we should always be very careful in distinguishing between what is called symbolism and what are the natural actions of things. Because when you light a fire, the flame of fire is not the symbol of fire—it is fire. So a symbol is like an equation in algebra, and it is part of the shape and form of the thing, which it represents and is a part of. A simple proof is that you can't draw a round circle and say, "This is the symbol of a square." It doesn't work. So that's my brief lesson about color.

Aloha and Vaya con Dios,
Victor

A Prayer for the Craft Neophyte

A Prayer for the Craft Neophyte

by Victor H. Anderson

I've read recently in certain "do-it-yourself" books on Witchcraft that one should recite the Lord's Prayer backwards while standing nude before a candle during the full moon. I've often been asked about this. I'm neither a "black" nor a "white" Witch. I'm a Witch and high priest of the Old Religion. I will be either/or as the need arises, but I dislike nastiness in any form. I do NOT practice inverted Christianity. If a good Christian prayer doesn't mise [sic] my beliefs, I will use it. However, there is a very good prayer that will release the neophyte from old inhibitions. Before I give it, I must explain its origin and what it is. I must confess to a very strange feeling since it used to be secret. It is our Lady's wish, so I don't give it lightly.

In a past incarnation close to this one, I was a Kahuna high priest in Hawai'i. Our training was long and hard. The initiation was quite elaborate and very ritualistic: both solemn and happy, culminating in feasting, dancing, and lovemaking as the Kahuna (new priest) was introduced to the *ali'i* (chiefs), the nobility, and other casts of people. Today, much of the grandeur is gone, to which we must bid a sad and fond aloha. Yet when I see a rainbow, I still feel the old strong Gods smiling upon me.

I hope that you have read the books by Max Freedom Long on Hawaiian magick or Huna. I highly recommend them to all Craft members. I grieve to see his wonderful work neglected. Witchcraft and Kahuna once shared the same great secret. Huna itself means "secret." I was given this knowledge when I was first initiated years ago, long before Mr. Long made his researches public. The myths and rotes of Witchcraft all reveal the "secret" to be but a thin veil for plain seeing. Even in our creation myths—if we understand the word "myth" as Robert Graves does—the Great Goddess and Her Consort often play the part of the human soul in its cycles of birth, death, and rebirth. In the grand myth of how the Goddess descended into the under-world to receive Death's scourge, and rise again, She plays the part of the soul, both male and female. This was once withheld from the uninitiated, but hopefully we're living in a more enlightened age.

Originally, Kahuna and other Old Religion traditions, taught that the human being has not just one soul or spirit, but three. These are, in Hawaiian, the *Unihipili* ("subconscious mind"), *Uhane* (conscious mind), and *Aumakua* (Personal God).

When I was living in Hawai'i, and during my initiation into Witchcraft in this incarnation, the introduction to Aumakua was one of the first steps taken after the vows of secrecy. They had another word for it, which I'm still asked to keep secret. I am permitted to say that it was sometimes called the Blue God. The grand myth has other meanings, but I cannot discuss them as they concern nature mysteries and things of a hidden nature.

Witchcraft teaches that the Cosmic Conscious, or Universal, is everywhere. We teach that, in its Greek sense, it is atomic in nature. These "atoms" of consciousness and reality, are the monads or *atmas*. In my instruction, I often compare the Universal to a great sea of light. Each of us is made up of four monads. The two lower selves are one monad each. The so-called subconscious self uses the vital body as its vehicle. The "conscious mind" uses the auric, or mental, body as its vehicle. In normal states, both these bodies are blended together, the auric body surrounding the vital body. The God-self is a pair of monads in one etheric body and is of dual sex. It dwells outside the other bodies and is attached to the lower self by means of a kind of etheric cord. Much of real magick consists of training the so-called subconscious self not to be afraid of a Personal God (due to the many complexes and guilt feelings we fall heir to as humans). It must learn enough self-confidence to reach out along the silver cord and touch the God-self so that our prayers may be received and answered by it, or passed on to the Gods for needed help. The Goddess teaches the Witch that in order for her or him to make successful contact with the higher beings, all three selves must be functioning properly on each of their own levels.

Understanding the above, it should be easy for the Witchcraft neophyte to use the following prayer. Two candles should be used, one blue, the other white. Tall candles are best. When the moon is full, remove all clothing and place the candles so that the blue one is to the left and the white one to the right. Have the prayer written so that you can chant it three times using mostly a single note. Take four deep breaths. Exhale. Wait a few moments and take another four deep breaths. Then recite the prayer. As you do, visualize in your mind's eye how the electric-blue fire is burning away old fears and anxieties. This is a positive ritual. Reciting the Lord's Prayer backwards is negative and not part of true Wicca. Work this ritual and it will work for you:

Prayer for Beginning the New Path

Our Father-Mother Spirit who dwells
In the Aka world of light above,
We call upon you, honoring and hallowing your name.
Create the perfect answers to this prayer
First in the Aka world above,
Then suddenly materialize and solidify them
Into immediate realities here and now on the earth plane
Even as they are where you have first created them.
Give us this day our daily bread and all of which it is a part.
Forgive us our sins at the same time we forgive
      those who have sinned against us,
But withhold not forgiveness from us,
For we are in most need of you.
Let not the Aka cord to you be loose,
And let us not be caught in a snare.
But deliver us from evil, for we know,
You are utterly trustworthy, kind, good and beautiful
And will always and ever be so.
Shine down into your lower selves the light
And give us perfect union with you, our Highest Self.
Amene sila!

(Victor H. Anderson)

First published in Witchcraft Digest Magazine, *no. 2 (New York: Witches Anti-Defamation League and* WICA, *1972): 13–14.*

The New Biography of
Victor Anderson

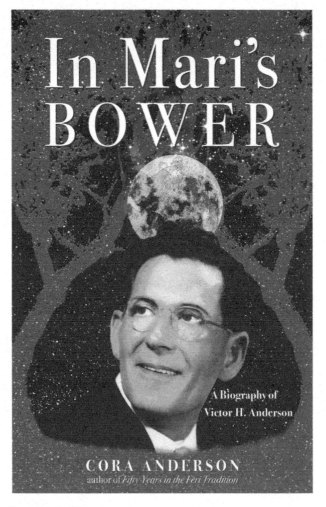

Paperback, 96 pages
$13.95 (CAN $15.95)
978-1-936863-77-8
http://harpybooks.com/Order/

The Classic Book of Love and Craft Poetry

Thorns of the Blood Rose
Paperback, 106 pages
$12.00 (CAN $13.95)
978-0-9710050-3-7
http://harpybooks.com/Order/

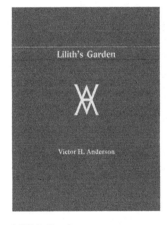

The Further Poetry of Victor Anderson

Lilith's Garden
Paperback, 87 pages
$12.00 (CAN $13.95)
978-0-9710050-5-1
http://harpybooks.com/Order/

H
HARPY
BOOKS

What Every Witch
Should Know

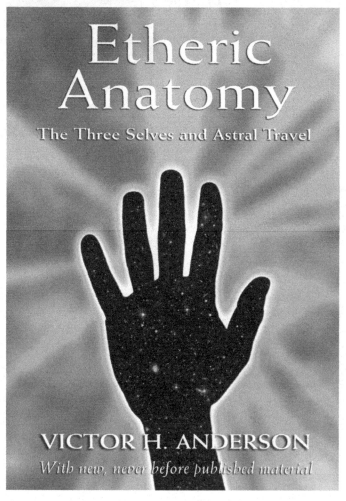

Etheric
Anatomy
The Three Selves and Astral Travel

VICTOR H. ANDERSON
With new, never before published material

Paperback, 112 pages
$12.00 (CAN $13.95)
978-0-9710050-0-6
http://harpybooks.com/Order/

HARPY
BOOKS

*An Inspiring Recollection from
a Beloved Craft Elder*

"A wise woman who walked the Path."–Mary K. Greer, author of *Women of the Golden Dawn*

Kitchen Witch

a Memoir

Cora Anderson

Author of *Fifty Years in the Feri Tradition*

Paperback, 168 pages
$14.95 (CAN $16.95)
978-0-9710050-7-5
http://harpybooks.com/Order/

HARPY
BOOKS

The Definitive Text on
the Feri Tradition

Paperback, 64 pages
$10.00 (CAN $11.95)
978-0-9710050-4-4
http://harpybooks.com/Order/

HARPY
BOOKS